The Hurt

by
Teddi Doleski

Illustrated by William Hart McNichols

paulist press

To
my parents
and to
Justin and Jason

Justin and Gabriel were friends. They played together almost every day.

One day Gabriel got mad at Justin. He said,
"Justin, you are a pig-faced punk."

Justin didn't know what to say. He walked away from Gabriel and went into his own house.

He was hurt. The Hurt was like a big round stone, all cold and hard. It seemed he could hold it in his hand and feel the hardness.

Justin didn't tell anybody how he felt. He took the Hurt into his room.

Gabriel isn't my friend anymore, he thought.
The Hurt grew bigger.

I'll never talk to him again, he thought. I'll
just stay here in my own room by myself.
The Hurt grew even bigger.

Justin heard Daddy call him.

He was happy that Daddy was home. He ran out to see him.

Daddy said, "Justin, I'm very disappointed in you. You tracked mud into the house. Just look at the floor."

Justin went back to his room. Daddy didn't even notice that I put away my hat, he thought. Daddy only notices the bad things I do. The Hurt was huge now. It was bigger than Justin.

Each day after that, Justin saved up all his bad feelings and gave them to the Hurt. The Hurt grew bigger and bigger.

Justin didn't really like the Hurt. It wasn't
as much fun as Gabriel. But the Hurt was
dependable. Justin didn't have to worry that
it would be nice one day and mean the next.
It was always the same, only bigger.

On Saturdays, Daddy helped Justin clean his room. They put away all the toys and folded the clothes.

They dusted and ran the vacuum cleaner and put clean sheets on the bed.

But this Saturday, Justin said, "I'll clean my room by myself, Daddy."
"OK," said Daddy. "I guess you're getting to be a big boy now. You don't need any help."

Justin didn't feel very big. He felt small.

But he didn't want Daddy to come into his room and see the Hurt. It was enormous now. There was hardly even room for Justin.

He felt lonely cleaning the room by himself.

That night as Justin slept, he felt the hard cold Hurt pushing against him.

When he awoke, he said, "My bed isn't snug anymore. That Hurt is ruining everything. Pretty soon it will be so big that there won't be room for me in here."

"Then there won't be room for me in the house."

"Then there won't be room for me in the world. The Hurt will take up all the space." Justin got scared.

"Daddy," Justin said. Daddy was making breakfast in the kitchen. "Daddy, a big Hurt came to live in my room, and it's taking up all the space."

"Where did it come from?" Daddy asked.

"It came from Gabriel calling me a bad name."

"What name?" asked Daddy.

"A pig-faced punk," said Justin. Saying the bad name out loud made him feel better.

"I understand why you were hurt," said Daddy. "Did you tell Gabriel how you felt?"

"No," said Justin. "I just came home."

Daddy sat down, and Justin climbed into his lap.

"Sometimes our friends make us feel very bad," said Daddy. "And other times they make us feel good."

"Gabriel made me feel good when I had chicken pox," said Justin. "He drew me a funny picture that made me laugh."

"Friends are good to have," said Daddy.

"But what will I do with the Hurt?" asked
Justin.
"You'll have to let it go," Daddy said.
"It's too big to get out of my room now," said
Justin.
"When you're ready to let it go, it will be
small enough."

When Justin went back to his room, the
Hurt was a little smaller.
"I don't want you here anymore, Hurt,"
Justin said. "You don't make a very good
friend."
The Hurt grew even smaller.

Justin went outside to help Daddy wash the car. He said, "Daddy, it hurt my feelings when you saw the mud I tracked in but you didn't see the hat I put away."

"I'm sorry," said Daddy. "You are very responsible about putting your things away. Sometimes I forget to tell you I'm proud of you. You're a fine little boy, and I'm glad you're my son."

Justin felt all sunshiny inside.

He wanted to make that car glisten. Working with Daddy was fun.

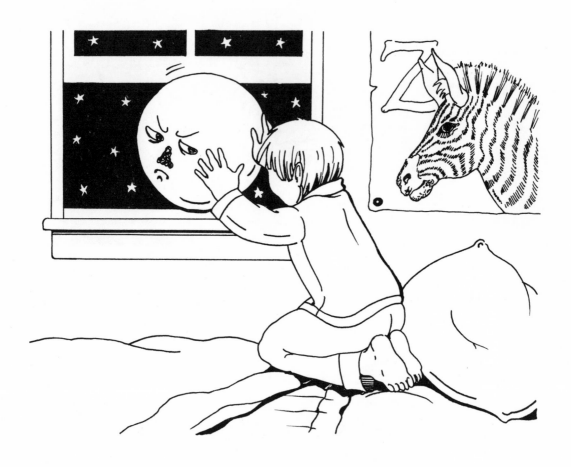

That night at bedtime, Justin opened his window. He pushed the Hurt to the window and left it there.

Then he went to bed. The bed felt warm and cozy.

In the morning the Hurt was gone.

Justin closed the window.

That day Justin went to Gabriel's house. "Do you want to play?" he asked.
"OK," said Gabriel.

From then on, they played together almost every day.

If Gabriel got mad and called Justin a pig-faced punk, Justin called Gabriel a crooked-eyed creep. Then they both laughed and went back to their playing.

Or sometimes, Justin would say, "Gabriel, I don't like it when you call me names." Gabriel would say, "I'm sorry." And Justin would say, "I forgive you." Then they would play some more.

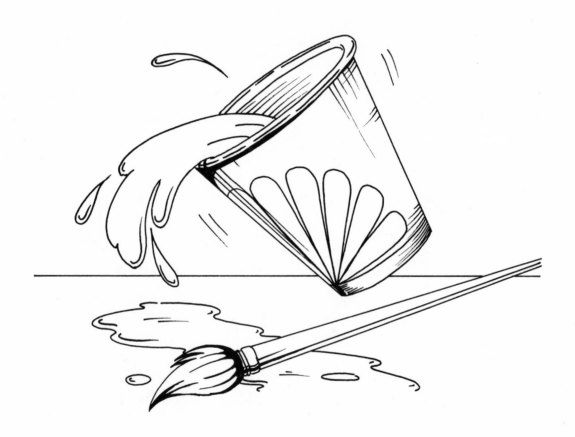

There were times when something bad would
happen, and the Hurt would come back.

But Justin didn't hide it. And he always let
it go before it got big.